Praying at Mass

Juliette Levivier

Illustrations by Anne Gravier

CTS Children's Books

Table of Contents

God calls his children together

God speaks to his children

Praying at Mass: Published 2008 by The Incorporated Catholic Truth Society, 40-46 Harleyford Road, London SE11 5AY. Tel: 020 7640 0042; Fax: 020 7640 0046; www.cts-online.org.uk. Copyright © 2008 The Incorporated Catholic Truth Society in this English-language edition. Translated from the French edition by Helena Scott.

ISBN: 978 1 86082 491 3   CTS Code CH 11

Jesus gives us his life

Jesus sends us out to our brothers and sisters

Nihil obstat: The Reverend Canon John Redford S.T.L., L.S.S., D.D.
Imprimatur: ✠ Peter Smith, Archbishop of Southwark, 23 May 2011.

The Nihil obstat and Imprimatur are a declaration that a book or pamphlet is considered to be free from doctrinal or moral error. It is not implied that those who have granted the Nihil obstat and Imprimatur agree with the contents, opinions or statements expressed.

Prier à la messe by Juliette Levivier, illustrations by Anne Gravier, published 2007 by Edifa-Mame, 15-27 rue Moussorgski, 75018 Paris; ISBN Edifa 978-2-9163-5013-4; ISBN Mame 978-2-7289-1220-9. Copyright © Edifa Mame 2007.

How happy I was
when they told me
"Let's go to God's house!"

(from Psalm 122)

God calls his
children together

The bells ring

Ding, dong! The bells of the church are ringing out!
Ding! It's Sunday!
Dong! Wake up, everybody! Wake up!
Ding! It's time for Mass!
Dong! Come on, everyone!
Ding! The Lord is calling you!
Dong! Quick, everyone!

The bells call us to go and see the Lord and to gather around him. I get ready as fast as I can – we mustn't be late for our meeting with Jesus...

I look smart and clean all over. Jesus is waiting to see me, I'm going to meet him. Sunday is such an important day!

Lord, I know you're waiting for me.
On the way to meet you
I get ready to listen to your words,
to receive your life, to share your peace!
I'm coming, Lord!

The Church, my family

Have you ever looked at the main doors of a big church? They sometimes have beautiful stone statues. In the middle is Christ: he is the one who gathers us together. Around him, you may see Our Lady, people from the Bible, and saints. They welcome us and remind us that the whole Church in heaven is with us in our prayer.

On the way in, I dip my fingers into the holy water and carefully make the sign of the Cross. That makes me think of the water that was poured on my forehead when I was baptised.

The Church, the family of God's children, is my family. The Church is God's house, it's the house of all the baptised, it's my house.

I'm not a Christian all on my own, Lord!
Ever since I was baptised I have
belonged to your people,
I'm a member of your Church.
Together with my brothers and sisters,
with them and for them,
I pray to you, Lord.
It's you, Lord, who gathers us all together.
In the name of the Father, and of the Son,
and of the Holy Spirit.

Let's sing for the Lord!

When we all sing with one voice, we are raising up to heaven the joy we feel at being gathered together in the name of Jesus Christ.

It's so beautiful to hear! There are deep voices and high ones, clear voices and rough ones... There are even some that sing a little out of tune!

Meanwhile the priest and altar-servers are coming in a procession. They join their voices to ours: yes, we really are just one single people.

Singing is a very beautiful way of praying!

I love singing! I follow the words on a sheet of paper or in a book. My voice, blending with everyone else's, rises up to the Lord.

Children of men, bless the Lord!
Priests of the Lord, bless the Lord!
Servants of the Lord, bless the Lord!
Sing to him, thank him,
for his love is everlasting!

(from the Canticle of Daniel)

Lord, have mercy!

We prepare to meet God by recognising our sins and by telling him we're sorry.

I commit sins:
in my thoughts: when I think unkind things about other people,
in my words: when I say things that hurt others,
in what I have done: when I am naughty and do wrong,
and in what I have failed to do: when I don't do the good things that I could.

We sing, "Lord, have mercy! Christ, have mercy!" Sometimes we say, "Kyrie, eleison! Christe, eleison!" That's Greek, the language the Gospels were written in, and it means the same thing.

I often fail to love God or my brothers and sisters. But I know that I can rely on the Lord to forgive me.

O God,
I have sinned against you
and against my brothers and sisters,
but I come to you for forgiveness.

May almighty God
have mercy on us,
forgive us our sins,
and bring us to everlasting life.

Amen.

Glory to God!

When Jesus was born, the angels in heaven sang at the top of their voices, "Glory to God in the highest, and peace to his people on earth" (Luke 2:14).

Today, at Mass, we praise him, we sing to him because he is the greatest person of all, and because his love is infinite. We are so happy to be his children, so happy to be together singing the glory of God our Father, his Son Jesus, and the Holy Spirit!

Then the priest says, "Let us pray." Listen carefully! It's a very short prayer, but a very beautiful one.

It is a specially joyful part of the Mass. Sometimes there's even some beautiful music at this point. Sing with all your heart to express your joy!

W e praise you,
we bless you,
we adore you,
we glorify you,
we give you thanks for your great glory,
Lord God, heavenly King,
O God, almighty Father.
For you alone are the Holy One,
you alone are the Lord,
you alone are the Most High,
Jesus Christ,
with the Holy Spirit,
in the glory of God the Father.

Amen.

Your word, O Lord,
is a lamp for my steps.
Your word, O Lord,
is a light for my path.

(From Psalm 119)

God speaks
to his children

What do you want
to say to me, Lord?

I sit down to listen to God speaking to me.

First a passage from the Old Testament. Jesus himself read those same passages, which tell us how God prepared mankind to receive him.

Then we respond to God with a psalm. These are very ancient prayers taken from the Bible. More singing! We all repeat the chorus together.

After that we read part of a letter written by one of the Apostles, or a passage about the beginnings of the Church.

If I listen carefully, I'm sure that there is something I can keep in my heart.

Your word, O Lord, is truth.
Your word is love.
Your word is light in the night.
Your word is the source of life.
Open my ears, Lord,
and above all, open my heart!

Alleluia, Jesus is alive!

All together we sing "Alleluia!" This time it's a Hebrew word, from Jesus' language, meaning "Praise God!"

Ever since Jesus rose from the dead, it's been a song of joy and victory, because we know that Jesus is alive among us, and that he gives us his word: the Gospel.

I stand up to show that I'm ready to follow Jesus. Sometimes there are grown-ups in front of me so I can't see. Luckily I can still hear!

The priest reads the Gospel. That's another strange word! It means "Good News". It's Jesus who brings us the Good News. He reveals to us that God loves us, he teaches us to love him in return, and he gives us his love.

The Gospel tells me how much Jesus loves me, and how he lived. What can I do to be like him?

A little cross on my forehead
to understand everything
that you tell me, Lord!
A little cross on my mouth
to talk about you, Lord!
A little cross on my heart
to love as you love, Lord!

21

Living by the Gospel
every day

Everyone sits down, and the priest explains to us how we can understand the Word of God that we have just heard, to know God better and to live more in his love.
Being Christian in everything that we do and in everything that we say, isn't always easy...

And what about me? How can I love Jesus more? At home, at school, with the people I like and the ones I don't like so much, I need to live by the Gospel. I believe it really is possible, with the help of Jesus and the Holy Spirit!

If you find the homily a bit long, look up. Look how the light shines through the stained-glass windows. They often tell stories from the Bible, the life of Jesus or the lives of the saints. It's very useful for people who can't read!

I want to talk!
Look, Jesus, I offer you my silence.

I want to wriggle about!
Look, Jesus, I offer you my patience.

I want to go out!
Look, Jesus, I offer you my presence here.

I believe

Now I stand up again to proclaim my faith.

I'm not sure what all the words mean, but I know that God
loves me and I love him, and so:
with everyone who is here at Mass,
with everyone who believes that God loves us,
with everyone who believes that Jesus is the Saviour,
the Son of God,
with everyone who trusts in the Holy Spirit,
with everyone who loves the Church,
with all the Christians in the world,
I say aloud, "I believe in God..."

When I say "I believe", I am united to the whole
Church. We have received the same Baptism, we hold
the same faith, we love the same God – yes, we really
are all brothers and sisters!

credo

I believe

je crois

I believe in God, the Father Almighty,
creator of heaven and earth.
I believe in Jesus Christ,
his only Son, our Lord…
I believe in the Holy Spirit,
the holy Catholic Church…
and life everlasting.

Amen.

creio

creo

ich glaube

Let us pray together
for the whole world

With all of the Church, I pray for the whole world. But the world is so big! How can we pray for so many people? To meet all those people we don't need to get on an aeroplane, we don't need to go on a long journey. Jesus has given us a very simple way of meeting them: in prayer. By praying like this, I am helping my heart grow bigger, and I am doing what Jesus asked us to do: praying for one another.

Together, we pray for the Church.
Together, we pray for the world.
Together, we pray for those who are suffering.
Together, we pray for our parish community.

I think of the people I want to entrust to Jesus: my Grandma who is so tired, my friend who is ill, the lady who teaches me catechism classes, the children who live in countries at war...

For the Pope, for the bishops,
for the priests,
for the whole people of God,
we pray to you, Lord!

For peace in the world, we pray to you, Lord!

For the people who are ill,
people who are lonely,
people who are hungry, or cold, or afraid,
we pray to you, Lord!

27

For all the people
who are here,
for all the people
who don't believe,
we pray to you,
Lord!

Let us give thanks to the Lord,
for his love has no end!

(from Psalm 136)

Jesus
gives us
his life

Blessed are you, Lord
God of all creation

Now comes the preparation of the gifts. Sometimes there's a procession with children and grown-ups. Otherwise the altar-servers bring the bread and wine that the priest places on the altar.

Together with the bread and wine, we offer our own lives to God: our work, our joys, our sufferings, our efforts... and even our rest!

Meanwhile there's a collection. The coins jingle in my hand, and they make a nice noise when they drop into the basket. That money is also an offering: it represents the work of each person, and their sharing in the life of the Church.

Everything that I have, I've received from God. I thank him for everything he gives me...

Blessed are you, Lord God of all creation,
for through your goodness we have received
the bread we offer you:
fruit of the earth and work of human hands,
it will become for us the bread of life. 31

Blessed be God for ever.

This is my Body

The priest, in the name of Jesus, repeats the words he said at the last supper with his Apostles, just before his Passion. This is the Consecration. Then the bread really becomes the Body of Jesus, and the wine really becomes the Blood of Jesus.

Jesus is present in lots of different ways. He's present in his Word, in our hearts, in our brothers and sisters...
At Mass he is present in a very special way: in the Host, which is really his Body.

Everyone stands up, or kneels down, as a sign of great respect and adoration.

The priest lifts up the Host, and then the Chalice. Jesus is there, in front of me. I look at him.

During the last meal
that Jesus shared with his disciples,
he took bread, and gave you thanks,
and shared the bread
with his friends, telling them:
"Take this, all of you, and eat of it:
for this is my Body,
which will be given up for you."
He also took the chalice of wine,
and gave you thanks,
and gave the chalice to his friends,
telling them: 33
"Take this, all of you, and drink from it,
for this is the chalice of my blood,
the blood of the new and eternal covenant,
which will be poured out for you and for many
for the forgiveness of sins."

The mystery of our faith is something really great!

The sacrifice of Jesus, who gave his life on the Cross to save us from death and sin, is made present in each Eucharist.

By his Passion and Resurrection, we have eternal life, and we believe that one day all people will be gathered together before God, in one single love.

The mystery of our faith is something really great!

At Mass, we celebrate all the wonders that God has accomplished because he loves everyone in the world and wants to save them all.

At each Mass, we welcome the Risen Jesus and we ask him to lead us to his Father.

We proclaim your Death, O Lord,
and profess your Resurrection
until you come again.

Jesus, I give myself to you

Because the Mass makes present the moment when Jesus gave up his life, we also can give ourselves to his Father, and entrust everyone in the world to him.

This is why the priest prays for the whole world, for the Church, the Pope, the bishops, and all of us.

He also prays that Jesus will welcome into his Kingdom the people who have died.

At this point in the Mass, you can give your life to Jesus and entrust to him all the people you know, whether they are close to you or far away.

Lord, come to the help
of our Pope, our Bishop,
all priests, and all your people.
I also pray to you for the people I love
and the people I don't love enough.
Remember the people who have died.
Welcome them lovingly into your house.

Our Father

One day, his disciples asked Jesus: "Lord, teach us to pray."

Then Jesus taught them a very simple prayer, which we love to say all together. Everywhere in the whole world, millions of Christians pray in the same words.

Jesus himself told us that we can call God our Father, just as he did.

How lovely it is to be able to call God "Daddy!"

Even my Dad is a child of God, even the priest who celebrates Mass, even that old lady over there! I can say this beautiful prayer together with them, and with all Christians.

Our Father,
who art in heaven,
hallowed be thy name.
Thy kingdom come.
Thy will be done on earth
as it is in heaven.
Give us this day our daily bread,
and forgive us our trespasses,
as we forgive those
who trespass against us,
and lead us not into temptation,
but deliver us from evil.

Amen.

Blessed are those who are called to the Lord's Supper!

Now comes the moment when you receive the peace of Jesus, and give a kiss, a handshake, or a smile to your neighbours, your Mum, your big sister... It's great to live in the peace of God!

Then the priest, raising up the Host, repeats the words said by St John the Baptist when he pointed Jesus out to his disciples:

"Behold the Lamb of God,

behold him who takes away the sins of the world.

Blessed are those called to the supper of the Lamb."

Everyone responds:

"Lord, I am not worthy

that you should enter under my roof,

but only say the word

and my soul shall be healed."

If you've made your First Holy Communion, and you are properly prepared, walk forward reverently to receive the Body of Christ. If not, you can cross your hands on your heart and go up to receive our Lord's blessing. Either way, you answer "Amen."

"Amen" means: "It's true, I agree, I believe that Jesus lives in me."

Father, you love us so much:
let us come to your table,
united in the joy of the Holy Spirit,
to receive the Body and Blood of your Son.

Thank you, Lord!

How quiet it is all of a sudden! Nobody is moving, or singing. Everyone is praying quietly. It's not a time for fidgeting!

Jesus is here, in each one of us. He gives us his strength, his peace, so that we can live by his love every day of the week.

So everyone is thanking Jesus with all their heart for giving them so much, for loving them so much.

How beautiful it is to receive Jesus and welcome him... I pray to him in silence, to thank him for this wonderful gift and to entrust everyone I love to his care. His infinite love fills me with happiness.

My Lord and my God!

Blessed be the name of
the Lord for ever and ever!

Lord Jesus,
by this Holy Communion
you have come to your home.
I want to say thank you
with all my heart
for making your home in me.

The Lord works marvels for me,
holy is his name!

Sing a new song to the Lord!
Sing to the Lord, all the earth!
Proclaim his love day by day,
and tell his wonders among all the peoples!

(from Psalm 96)

Jesus sends us
out to our
brothers and sisters

Go in the peace of Christ!

When we have shared in the Eucharist, we go away full of strength, peace and joy.

This peace that lives in us doesn't come from ourselves, it comes from the Holy Spirit. Jesus tells us today what he told his disciples: "I leave you peace, my peace I give you." Not to keep it for ourselves – no! To give it to all the people we meet, today, tomorrow, and every day of the week.

46

When I'm at home and when I'm at school, Jesus asks me to live by his love and peace, which I have received and shared at Mass. He asks me to spread his love and peace around me, to the people I love but also to the people I don't like so much.

help

But... haven't we finished?
The priest starts speaking again.
He tells us what's going to happen in
the parish this week: catechism classes,
prayer groups, funerals, weddings...

I'm dying to get up. My legs are already moving, they
want to go and take the peace of Jesus everywhere!
But parish life is very important: there are lots of
things happening during the week!

I'm not a Christian all by myself in my little corner!
I belong to a community: I bring it my joy, my happiness,
my help, my prayer...

Life goes on

I can see the priest, he's saying hello to everyone!
And my Grandma!
And my friends from the catechism class!

We are all so happy to meet each other and say hello to people! Our parish really is a family: we live by the love that Jesus has come to put into our hearts.
All day long, all week long, we will live with the joy of Jesus, and we'll go and take it to others.

"Go out into the whole world, make disciples of all nations," he tells us.
The whole world?
How about beginning with my family?
All nations?
How about beginning with my friends?
Quick, quick, let's go out and play, life is great!